9/18

CUSTOMS AND CULTURES OF THE WORLD

MY TEENAGE LIFE IN BRAZIL

CUSTOMS AND CULTURES OF THE WORLD

My Teenage Life in AUSTRALIA

My Teenage Life in BRAZIL

My Teenage Life in CHINA

My Teenage Life in EGYPT

My Teenage Life in GREECE

My Teenage Life in INDIA

My Teenage Life in JAPAN

My Teenage Life in MEXICO

My Teenage Life in NEPAL

My Teenage Life in RUSSIA

My Teenage Life in SOUTH AFRICA

Our Teenage Life in the NAVAJO NATION

CUSTOMS AND CULTURES OF THE WORLD

MY TEENAGE LIFE IN BRAZIL

By Jim Whiting

with Lucca Passos

Series Foreword by
Kum-Kum Bhavnani

MASON CREST

Mason Crest
450 Parkway Drive, Suite D
Broomall, PA 19008
www.masoncrest.com

Printed and bound in the United States of America.

First printing
9 8 7 6 5 4 3 2 1

Series ISBN: 978-1-4222-3899-8
ISBN: 978-1-4222-3901-8
ebook ISBN: 978-1-4222-7880-2

Library of Congress Cataloging-in-Publication Data
Names: Whiting, Jim, 1943- author. | Passos, Lucca, author.
Title: My teenage life in Brazil / by Jim Whiting with Lucca Passos ; series foreword by Kum-Kum Bhavnani.
Description: Broomall, PA : Mason Crest, 2018. | Series: Customs and cultures of the world | Includes index.
Identifiers: LCCN 2017003257| ISBN 9781422239018 (hardback) | ISBN 9781422278802 (ebook)
Subjects: LCSH: Brazil--Social life and customs--Juvenile literature. | Teenagers--Brazil--Social life and customs--Juvenile literature.
Classification: LCC F2508.5 .W48 2018 | DDC 305.2350981--dc23
LC record available at https://lccn.loc.gov/2017003257

Developed and Produced by Shoreline Publishing Group.
Editor: James Buckley, Jr.
Design: Tom Carling, Carling Design Inc.
Production: Sandy Gordon
www.shorelinepublishing.com

Front cover: Dreamstime.com/Chris Schmid

QR Codes disclaimer:

CONTENTS

Key Icons to Look For

Words to Understand: These words with their easy-to-understand definitions will increase the reader's understanding of the text, while building vocabulary skills.

Sidebars: This boxed material within the main text allows readers to build knowledge, gain insights, explore possibilities, and broaden their perspectives by weaving together additional information to provide realistic and holistic perspectives.

Educational Videos: Readers can view videos by scanning our QR codes, providing them with additional educational content to supplement the text. Examples include news coverage, moments in history, speeches, iconic sports moments, and much more!

Text-Dependent Questions: These questions send the reader back to the text for more careful attention to the evidence presented here.

Research Projects: Readers are pointed toward areas of further inquiry connected to each chapter. Suggestions are provided for projects that encourage deeper research and analysis.

Series Glossary of Key Terms: This back-of-the-book glossary contains terminology used throughout this series. Words found here increase the reader's ability to read and comprehend higher-level books and articles in this field.

SERIES FOREWORD

Culture: Parts = Whole

Culture makes us human.

Many of us think of culture as something that belongs to a person, a group, or even a country. We talk about the food of a region as being part of its culture (tacos, pupusas, tamales, and burritos all are part of our understanding of food from Mexico, and South and Central America).

We might also talk about the clothes as being important to culture (saris in India, kimonos in Japan, hijabs or *gallibayas* in Egypt, or beaded shirts in the Navajo Nation). Imagine trying to sum up "American" culture using just examples like these! Yet culture does not just belong to a person or even a country. It is not only about food and clothes or music and art, because those things by themselves cannot tell the whole story.

Culture is also about how we live our lives. It is about our lived experiences of our societies and of all the worlds we inhabit. And in this series—Customs and Cultures of the World—you will meet young people who will share their experiences of the cultures and worlds they inhabit.

How does a teenager growing up in South Africa make sense of the history of apartheid, the 1994 democratic elections, and of what is happening now? That is as integral to our world's culture as the ancient ruins in Greece, the pyramids of Egypt, the Great Wall of China, the Himalayas above Nepal, and the Amazon rain forests in Brazil.

But these examples are not enough. Greece is also known for its financial uncertainties, Egypt is known for the uprisings in Tahrir Square, China is known for its rapid development of megacities, Australia is known for its amazing animals, and Brazil is known for the Olympics and its football [soccer] team. And there are many more examples for each nation, region, and person, and some of these examples are featured in these books. The question is: How do you, growing up in a particular country, view your own culture? What do you think of as culture? What is your lived experience of it? How do you come to understand and engage with cultures that are not familiar to you? And, perhaps most importantly, why do you/we want to do this? And how does reading about and experiencing other cultures help you understand your own?

It is perhaps a cliché to say culture forms the central core of our humanity and our dignity. If that's true, how do young adults talk about your own cultures? How do you simultaneously understand how people apparently "different" from you live their lives, and engage with their cultures? One way is to read the stories in this series. The "authors" are just like you, even though they live in different places and in different cultures. We communicated with these young writers over the Internet, which has become the greatest gathering of cultures ever. The Internet is now central to the culture of almost everyone, with young people leading the way on how to use it to expand the horizons of all of us. From those of us born in earlier generations, thank you for opening that cultural avenue!

Let me finish by saying that culture allows us to open our minds, think about worlds different from the ones we live in, and to imagine how people very different from us live their lives. This series of books is just the start of the process, but a crucial start.

I hope you enjoy them.

—Kum-Kum Bhavnani
Professor of sociology and feminist and global studies at the University of California, Santa Barbara, and an award-winning international filmmaker.

MEET LUCCA!

I was born in São Paulo and moved to Salvador Bahia. I love to go skateboarding and surfing so that's one reason I picked Santa Barbara, California (below), for a year when I was an exchange student.

Editor's note: Lucca was interviewed while he was spending a year in Santa Barbara, California, as an exchange student.

SÃO PAULO!

To: The Reader

Subject: About Me!

I have two twin brothers, one year younger than me. One of my brothers is autistic. He is really good, but I miss him a lot [when I was in Santa Barbara]. My father is a businessman, and my mother works in a bank.

My mother's family is from São Paulo and I go there often to visit them. I prefer Salvador now, I'm used to it and it's a bit quieter than São Paulo.

I think I'd like to get into some sort of business, perhaps go to university in the US and go back to Brazil and start a business. Having an education from America will be very well respected when I go back home.

I spent my junior year in Santa Barbara, California, as an exchange student. I learned a lot there and really enjoyed my time in the US!

Brazil : An Introduction

For many years, people believed that the Nile River in Egypt and other parts of Africa was the world's longest. However, in 2007, a team of Brazilian scientists said that the Amazon deserved that honor because they claimed they had discovered a new and longer starting point for the mighty river. At 4,250 miles (6,839 km) in length, they said it was about 90 miles (144 km) longer than the Nile, though that measurement has not yet been widely accepted.

However, there is no question that the Amazon and its dozens of **tributaries** in Brazil and some of its neighbors—collectively known as the Amazon Basin—comprise the world's largest river system. Almost everything about the Amazon Basin staggers the imagination:

Words to Understand

amenities   features providing convenience, comfort, or pleasure

inadvertently   by mistake, without intention

indigenous   original; native to a place

stigma   mark of disgrace, set of negative beliefs

tributaries   rivers or streams flowing into a larger river

- Its total volume is about 75 times greater than the Nile.

- It accounts for one-fifth of the world's total freshwater flow into the ocean.

- It is home to at least 10 percent of all living species in the world.

- It occupies about 40 percent of the total area of the continent of South America.

- Half of the world's remaining rainforest lies within the Amazon Basin.

- During the rainy season the increased flow of water makes the Amazon River more than 30 miles (48.2 km)wide in some points.

- One of the islands in the Amazon Delta—the area where the river spreads out as it flows into the Atlantic Ocean—is larger than Switzerland.

Because all of these superlatives, nothing says "Brazil" more than the Amazon Basin. More than 80 percent of it lies in Brazil, which is by far the largest country in South America and the fifth-largest in the world. It could hold a dozen copies of Texas. Except for Chile and Ecuador, every South American country shares a border with Brazil. It is also one of just 12 countries with territory in both the Northern and Southern Hemispheres, though most of it is in the Southern Hemisphere. That means that its seasons are the opposite of those in the Northern Hemisphere.

Brazil is home to the Amazon rain forest, the largest in the world.

Other Regions

There's more to Brazil than the Amazon Basin. The Brazilian Plateau, which covers most of the eastern, central, and southern parts of the country, accounts for about half of Brazil's total area. Much of it consists of woodlands and it frequently rises more than 2,000 feet (610 m). The southeast occupies only about 10 percent of the land area but contains more than 40 percent of Brazil's population and several of its largest cities.

Brazil also boasts one of the world's largest uninterrupted shorelines, stretching more than 4,500 miles (7,242 km) along the Atlantic Ocean. It consists of coral reefs, lagoons, dunes, and above all some of the world's most spectacular and best-known beaches.

The Portuguese Arrive

Beginning in the late 15th century, the Portuguese expanded their reach far beyond their home country, exploring the coast of Africa and venturing into the Indian and Pacific Oceans. Shortly after Columbus discovered the New World, Pope Alexander VI negotiated the Treaty of Torsedillas. It divided these newfound lands between Portugal and Spain along a line running from north to south through the Atlantic Ocean. Spain received everything to the west of that line, Portugal everything to the east. So when explorer Pedro Álvares Cabral splashed ashore in northeastern Brazil in 1500, he claimed the land for Portugal because it lay east of the line. As a result, nearly everyone in Brazil speaks a version of Portuguese called Brazilian Portuguese. It is the only country in the Americas where Portuguese is the main language.

Of course, indigenous people had already lived in Brazil for thousands of years. The newcomers began exploiting the country's natural resources, especially sugar cane and brazilwood, which was used to make

Slavery in North America is well known, but Brazil and other South American countries also imported millions of slaves from Africa.

red dye and gave its name to the new colony. They used the natives for all of the hard work. Many died from the harsh treatment they received. The Portuguese also **inadvertently** brought diseases for which the natives had no natural immunity. The native population numbers plummeted. To replace the native peoples, the Portuguese began importing slaves from Africa. Eventually more than four million crossed the Atlantic. That's at least 10 times the number of slaves brought to North America and nearly half the worldwide total.

Brazilian soldiers celebrated upon the declaration of their country's independence from Portugal in 1822.

Half a Century of Stability

In the early 19th century, Emperor Napoleon of France invaded Portugal. The Portuguese royal family fled to Brazil and ruled from there. Eventually they returned home, leaving Prince Pedro in charge of the colony. To their surprise, Pedro declared Brazil's independence on September 7, 1822. He became Emperor Pedro I of the Empire of Brazil.

Pedro returned to Portugal nine years later. His son Pedro II became emperor and ruled for 49 years. Many historians believe he was the best ruler in the country's history. Brazil was largely stable and prosperous during his reign. Pedro II officially abolished slavery in 1888. It was the last country in the Western Hemisphere to do that. But the move turned the country's upper class against him. It was one of the reasons they joined with the military to remove him from power the following year and declare a republic.

Two New Landmarks

In 1931, an immense statue of Jesus Christ was erected on the 2,300-foot (701 m) Corcovado Mountain, which overlooks the city of Rio de Janeiro. The statue is in the form of a cross, with the Christ standing on a pedestal and his arms stretched straight out to the sides. Christ the Redeemer, as the statue is known, is instantly recognized as symbol of both the city and the country and is often regarded as one of the New Seven Wonders of the World.

By that time, Rio de Janeiro had been the country's capital for many years. But Brazilians often dreamed of a new capital in the country's interior, where it would be more centrally located and free from the stigma of its colonial legacy. That dream became reality in 1960 when the planned city of Brasilia was established. It was so far into the interior that many building supplies had to be airlifted to the site.

Known as Cristo Redentor in Portuguese, the statue dominates the skyline.

Fordlandia

Henry Ford, the American owner of the Ford Motor Company, wanted a cheap source of rubber for his cars. So in 1928, he built Fordlandia, a small town in the Amazon jungle devoted to rubber production. It was modeled after American small towns, with **amenities** such as a golf course, swimming pool, and tennis courts. Things quickly went wrong. The Brazilian workers didn't like the steady diet of American food. Working standard American nine-to-five shifts in the jungle heat, rather than in the cooler early morning and evening, sapped their energy. Perhaps most basic, Ford hadn't consulted agricultural experts. Any of them would have told him that the land wasn't suitable for growing rubber trees. Fordlandia was a spectacular flop. It never produced a single pound of rubber.

The World Comes to Brazil

Brazil came to the forefront of worldwide consciousness when it hosted the FIFA World Cup in 2014. Matching 32 of the world's best national soccer teams, the World Cup is widely regarded as the most widely watched sports event in the world. The hosts had high hopes of winning but could only muster a fourth-place finish. The national team lost 7–1 to Germany, sending the soccer-mad country into months of sadness and wonder about the future of the sport.

By the time the World Cup ended, however, preparations were well underway for an even larger sports event: the 2016 Summer Olympics in Rio de Janeiro. It was the first time the Olympics had been held in South America. More than 11,000 athletes from 205 countries took part. Brazilian athletes took advantage of performing before the home fans to win seven gold medals, their most ever. By far the most important was the soccer gold medal. It was the first time Brazil had won Olympic gold, with superstar Neymar adding to his luster by converting the winning goal in the penalty kick phase after the hosts and Germany battled to a 1-1 tie in regulation time. The victory helped calm some of the fears that had come up after the World Cup defeat.

Brazilian superstar Neymar (right; players usually go by one name) battled Mexico on the way to leading his team to a much-needed Olympic gold medal in 2016.

Perhaps more importantly, the two fairly successful events helped present a more positive view of Brazil to the world. Things were not perfect, but the Brazilian peoples' outgoing and positive attitude played a part in making both events work, even as the country struggled with economic and political issues (see page 42). ✳

LUCCA'S SCHOOL LIFE

To: The Reader

Subject: My School Life

My school in Brazil is completely different than what I experienced in Santa Barbara. In Brazil, you can't pick any of your classes. They are all chosen for you. We don't have any options for any electives.

In Brazil, people who study in public schools are mostly poor and the schools are not as good. My family is able to send me to private Catholic school. Every day we have the same classes including Math, Physics, and Chemistry. We study Brazilian history most of the time, but we also study world history. We have English from an early age. I don't think that learning English was that hard. But I think you learning Portuguese would be harder!

Usually, the teachers come to our classes, rather than us moving from class to class. In Santa Barbara, we called the teachers Mr. or Miss…in Brazil, we use their first name. The principal is the only one we call Mister.

In Brazil, the school year starts in February and finishes in November. The seasons are reversed there, of course. So when I arrived in Santa Barbara in August, I was halfway through my junior year, so I repeated a bit of it and then finished. So when I go back, I'll start half of my senior year. Then I hope to come back to college here, too!

To: **The Reader**

Subject: **Getting into College**

In Brazil, I think it's much harder [than in the US]. It's very, very hard to get into a good college. Here, you can choose what day you want to take the SAT. In Brazil, we have one test, it's called NA (ENEM). This test happens once a year, at the same time for the whole country. We have two days of that, five hours or so a day, and it covers all the topics. We take that as a senior to see what college we can get into. In the US, if you don't do well on the SAT, you can try again and see if you can do better. In Brazil, we have one chance. It's very intense.

I prefer math and physics because I prefer numbers to words.

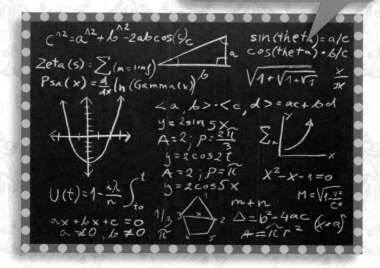

TIME TO EAT!

To: **The Reader**

Subject: **Eating**

In Brazil, we eat a lot of seafood, especially where I live, which is near the ocean. One typical food is called moqueca: Shrimp, clams, lobster mixed into a soup.

We have people who work in our apartment who help make the food. They are like our family, too. Many people I know have this.

The big meal is at lunch, not at dinner. At school, we start at 7 and then finish at 12. We go home and have a lunch with our whole family, including mom and dad. When I was younger, I went back to school. Now, in my final year, I only have classes a couple days a week in the afternoon.

Moqueca

Food in Brazil

As a nation that includes a wide diversity of people, Brazil boasts a very wide-ranging cuisine. Beef is very popular, especially in barbecue known as churrasco. Spanish influence is seen in the many rice and bean dishes, while the vast array of plants has created very flavorful and interesting side dishes.

However, as the country's population has increased along with access to increased food supplies, the government is trying to stem a rise in obesity. While Brazilians have a long way to go to match America's poor nutrition record, they are now approaching the levels of European obesity rates for the first time.

In 2016, the national government put out a food guide to help people make better choices—mostly to avoid processed foods and junk food. Among the key steps noted in the plan are to eat natural foods, avoid too much oil in cooking, cut down on packaged foods like cookies and snacks, and avoid fast-food restaurants. The plan received international praise when it was released.

Brazilian Culture

Brazil has long been noted for its "melting pot" nature. Descendants of the original Portuguese settlers form a large percentage of the population. Following the abolition of slavery, other Europeans and a significant number of Asians immigrated to Brazil. There has been considerable intermarriage with the descendants of the slaves. The impact of a large population of Africans forcibly moved here generations ago is also seen in the population. The result is a vibrant culture that draws from the traditions of all these groups.

Also, according to estimates, about 300,000 indigenous people from more than 200 tribes continue to live in the rain forest, where they have established a distinctive culture dating back many centuries. Some have little contact with the overall Brazilian culture. Sadly, those that have connected with the wider culture have often suffered. Many tribes of indigenous people have nearly disappeared as they assimilate into the wider culture.

Words to Understand

iconic   representing something of immense significance

telenovelas   popular soap opera-style dramatic programs broadcast on TV

More than 110,000 fans can pack Rio's largest stadium, the Maracanã, as shown here for a Brazilian league game.

"O País do Futebol"

When people think of Brazil, soccer (or football as it is known there) immediately comes to mind. Brazilians refer to themselves as "o País do Futebol" (the country of football) and more than 10,000 of them play professionally throughout the world. Players such as Ronaldinho (top players typically use just one name), Kaká, Neymar, and especially Pelé are household names. Brazil has won five World Cups (1958, 1962, 1970, 1994, 2002), more than any other country, and twice was second. It is also

the only team to have appeared in every World Cup. Losses such as the 1950 final to neighboring Uruguay and the 7–1 humiliation by Germany before the home fans in 2014 were occasions for national mourning. While Brazil has yet to win the Women's World Cup, the team boasts one runner-up and one third place finish. Longtime star Marta is often considered one of the world's best female soccer players.

Soccer fans especially enjoy the Brazilian style of play. Long ago they coined the term *o jogo bonito* ("the beautiful game") to describe the way they played. If games awarded style points, Brazilian teams would be at the top of the rankings. They play the game with exuberance, creativity, fast footwork, and continual attacking. Their yellow jerseys are among the most **iconic** uniforms in all of sports.

Besides the normal 11-on-11 game, Brazilians flock to the beach for 7-on-7 on the sand and play 5-on-5 games indoors, called *futsal* (literally "football in a room.") Another variation is footvolley, a two-person combination of soccer and volleyball that is another popular beach sport. Players can only use their feet and heads to get the ball over the net. For several years in the early 1970s, some Brazilians even played autobol, in which cars pushed around a ball that was four feet tall. Car crashes and broken bones were common and that soccer version didn't last.

Pelé

Many people regard Pelé as the greatest soccer player of all time. English star Sir Bobby Charlton said "I sometimes feel as though football was invented for this magical player." *Time* magazine named him one of the 100 most influential people of the 20th century. His real name is Edson Arantes do Nascimento, though it's not clear where his iconic nickname came from. Pelé grew up in poverty and began playing with a sock stuffed with newspaper and rags. He made rapid progress, turning pro in 1956 when he was just 15. He helped Brazil win its first World Cup two years later and spent nearly two decades as the world's most famous player. The two sides in the Nigerian Civil War even agreed to a 48-hour ceasefire when he played a match there. Today he serves as a global ambassador for humanitarian causes.

Americans and Europeans might have seen this growing Brazilian export—the martial art of capoeira, which mixes dance and flowing movements.

Other Sports

Many people believe that mixed martial arts (MMA) is the country's second-most-popular sport. Hélio Gracie founded Brazilian jiu-jitsu in the early 1900s. Its techniques helped small men like himself overcome their size handicap and defeat much larger opponents. "Carlos [his brother] and Hélio Gracie brought a fresh eye to jujitsu [which had originated in Japan] just as their fellow countryman brought a special new approach to football," writes one authority. Gracie's sons introduced the sport into the United States and helped it evolve into MMA, which is now a worldwide sport.

Basketball and volleyball also rank high in popularity. Basketball arrived in Brazil in 1894 and has experienced rapid growth in recent years. The women's national team won the world championship in 1994. The men's national team often finishes high in international tournaments, and more than a dozen Brazilians have played in the NBA. Anderson Varejao helped the Cleveland Cavaliers win the 2016 league title. The NBA encourages the growth of the sport by establishing Junior NBA programs for both boys and girls in Brazil.

The famous wide, white sands of Copacabana Beach in Rio de Janeiro draw sun-lovers from around the world.

The men's and women's national volleyball and beach volleyball teams have won numerous Olympic gold medals and world championships. Many experts say volleyball is the country's most popular sport among young girls.

Beach Boys and Girls

Going to world-famous beaches such as Rio de Janeiro's Copacabana and Ipanema—and countless numbers of lesser known but equally attractive ones—is an important part of Brazilian culture. In fact, beachgoing is so enjoyable that many workers head for the sand during their lunch breaks. One reason for this popularity is that beaches are open to everyone, regardless of their income level.

While swimming and sun-bathing are important, those aren't the only reasons to hit the sand. The beach is an ideal place to spend time with friends and family members, eat and drink, and participate in activities like pickup soccer, volleyball, and kite flying. It seems like everyone wears flip-flops, while men usually don boxer-style swimsuits (definitely not Speedos) and women are often clad in string bikinis.

Not all samba dancers are this well-costumed, but the dance is a huge part of Brazilian culture.

Music

Brazilians love music. The samba is the country's most notable music form, originating in Africa and crossing the Atlantic with the slaves who were imported to work in Brazil. While there are many forms of samba, they all have a pulsating rhythm that also lends itself to dancing. A popular offshoot called the bossa nova developed in Rio de Janeiro in the 1950s. Songs such as "Blame It on the Bossa Nova" reached the top levels of pop music charts throughout the world and helped familiarize Brazilian music to a much wider audience.

Brazilians, like people in several Latin American countries, love soap operas, called telenovelas. *More than 50 million people watched the final episode of this drama.*

The country's best-known classical composer is Heitor Villa-Lobos, often referred to as "the single most significant creative figure in 20th-century Brazilian art music." Most of his work, such as his Bachianas Brasileiras, emphasizes folk tunes and rhythms from Portugal, Africa, and indigenous Brazilians. Brazilians flock to free outdoor concerts featuring his music as well as other classical composers from Brazil and the rest of the world.

Telenovelas

Brazilians love to watch television. According to estimates, 97 percent of the population have TVs. The country's largest network, Rede Globo, has more stations than any other network in the world except ABC, CBS, and NBC in the United States. Only ABC has more annual revenue. The most popular shows are **telenovelas**. These are similar to American soap operas in the intensity of the emotions expressed by the characters and the complicated plots, which typically involve three parallel plots—one each from the upper, middle, and lower classes. Crossovers among these plots increase the complexity.

Unlike soaps, however, telenovelas almost always have a fixed duration, typically ranging from six months to a year. And as they near their conclusion, more than 90 percent of the total viewing audience is likely to tune in. ✳

Clip from a telenovela

LUCCA'S TOWN

Salvador de Bahia is not like the city of my birth, São Paulo, which is a huge place. Salvador Bahia (below) is more like a beach city. But it's still a city and we can't really go out and skate wherever we would like. It's kind of dangerous.

Here's a cool street music scene in Salvador.

To: The Reader

Subject: My Town

In Brazil, there are very few neighborhoods with small houses like in the United States. Most cities have lots of large apartment buildings. From my window, I can see many such buildings. I live in a building like that, with 30 floors, and we live on the 12th.

In Brazil, we have a law that when it's really late, you can run stop signs. It's literally too dangerous to stop your car that late at night. In America, you never see that. People in the US follow laws much more, I think.

Brazilian Customs

B esides sand, soccer, and the mighty sweep of the Amazon River, the Brazilian Carnival (*Carnaval* in Portuguese) also says "Brazil." It is the country's most famous festival and is also generally regarded as the world's largest. While the best-known celebration takes place in Rio de Janeiro and attracts millions of people—including hundreds of thousands of tourists—virtually every corner of the country has its own version of Carnaval.

Carnaval lasts for six days and is such an important part of Brazilian culture that hardly any businesses stay open. Its dates range from early February to early March, starting on the Friday before **Ash Wednesday** and concluding on Ash Wednesday, which marks the beginning of the Christian rite of Lent.

Words to Understand

Ash Wednesday   The first day of Lent in the Christian calendar. It occurs 46 days before Easter and includes 40 days of fasting, especially not eating meat (the six Sundays during this period are not fast days). Its name comes from the custom of using ashes to make the sign of the cross on worshippers' foreheads.

derisively   mocking, jeering

One of the highlights of Carnaval in Rio is the Samba-drome, a huge parade of samba dancing clubs that can take hours to pass by.

It is built around dancing and music, especially the samba. In Rio, long parades of samba school dancers are one of the main attractions. Participants often spend a full year preparing for the event. Carnaval is also characterized by the overturning of social conventions. Poor people dress as princes, the wealthy may wear castaway clothing, and men often dress as women and vice versa.

Carnaval Roots

The word "carnival" dates back nearly 600 years and is connected with the Catholic custom of Lent, when people are not supposed to eat meat. It comes from two Latin roots: *carne*, which means "meat" or "flesh," and *levare*, meaning "to raise" or "to remove." Eventually it took on the meaning of circus, carnival, or fair. Carne also occurs in words such as chili con carne ("chili pepper with meat"), carnage ("slaughter of the flesh of many people"), carnivorous ("eating meat"), and carnation (because the flower's reddish-pink color resembles the skin tone of many people). Levare forms the common word lever (which is used to help raise something and then remove it).

Honoring a Courageous Dentist

April 21 is Tiradentes Day. It honors Joaquim José da Silva Xavier. He was a leader of the Brazilian independence movement in the late 18th century, which sought complete independence from Portugal. He was captured and executed on April 21, 1792, after a trial lasting nearly three years. His opponents **derisively** referred to him during the trial as "Tiradentes," which means "tooth puller" and was an insult because dentists didn't have much status in that era. He was hanged then beheaded, and his body chopped into several pieces to terrorize the population. Nearly a century later his successors revived his memory to encourage their followers to work toward establishment of a Brazilian republic.

Like many countries throughout the world, Brazilians celebrate May 1 as Labor Day. It honors the achievements of the millions of Brazilian workers. Massive throngs of people take to the streets in parades that last for several hours. Perhaps most importantly, many businesses announce pay raises on that day.

Saints Days and More

The vast majority of Brazilians are Roman Catholic. Because of that, many of their popular holidays are tied to the church calendar. In June,

Brazilians celebrate Festas Junina. It marks the feast days of three saints: St. Anthony on June 12, Saint John on June 23, and St. Peter on June 28. It is a succession of mainly outdoor parties, with music, dancing, and lots of barbecued food. It also includes religious processions and fireworks. Because St. Anthony is the patron saint of single men and women, it's common to have mock weddings on his feast day.

Brazilians honor their servicemen and women on Soldier's Day on August 25. It was the birthdate of Luís Alves de Lima e Silva, also known as the Duke of Caxias, in 1803. Many authorities maintain that he was the country's greatest general. He defended Pedro II during several rebellions, then led Brazilian forces to victories in wars against their neighbors.

Some Festas Juninas celebrations can be colorful affairs, packed with dancing and decorated with pictures of the saints.

An honor guard of Brazilian cavalry, dressed in uniforms dating back to the 1800s, rides in an Independence Day parade.

One of the country's most cherished holidays is Independence Day, which falls on September 7. It honors Brazil's declaration of independence from Portugal in 1822. Parades in Brasilia and other major cities honor the country's servicemen and women and remind the people of their heritage.

November 15 marks another patriotic holiday, Republic Day. It recognizes the day in 1889 when Pedro II, the country's second emperor, had to step down and Marshal Deodoro da Fonseca said Brazil was now a republic. The date is also when people vote during election years.

A Great Catch

Another important holiday falls on October 12, and honors Our Lady of Aparecida, Brazil's patron saint. The festival dates back to October 1717. Three fishermen were down on their luck. Their catches were minimal every time they went out. In desperation, they prayed to the Virgin Mary. The next time they went out, they hauled up a clay statue of the Virgin Mary in their net. It was small, less than three feet tall. It probably dated back to about 1650 and had been submerged for decades. Afterward, they had no trouble catching fish. Their neighbors also venerated the statue because it provided good fortune to them as well. They quickly named it

Pilgrims wait in long lines to honor Brazil's patron saint, Our Lady of Aparecida. The huge basilica named for her is the second-largest church in the world.

Nossa Senhora Aparecida, which means "our lady who appeared," and built a small chapel.

Today, upwards of 45,000 people at a time honor Aparecida in the National Sanctuary of Our Lady of Aparecida in São Paolo. It is the second-largest church in the world—only St. Peter's Basilica in Vatican City is larger.

Like many other countries, Brazil celebrates All Souls' Day on November 2. People visit the gravesites of relatives and friends and decorate them with flowers and candles.

As in many countries, Christmas time is shopping time in Brazil. Malls go all out to attract shoppers with decorations like these ("Merry Christmas" in Portuguese).

Christmas and New Year's

Christmas is one of the most festive times of the year. Many traditions date back centuries to Portugal. One is a nativity scene called the *presépio*, which literally means "bed of straw." Brazilians use the name Papai Noel to mean Santa Claus. Many children leave empty shoes by open windows on Christmas Eve, hoping that Papai Noel will fill them with presents in the night. Because Brazil is in the Southern Hemisphere and December is early summer there, many people enjoy the holiday by going to one of Brazil's beaches.

The beaches also attract throngs for New Year's Eve, the final celebration of the year. Many people wear white, which is a symbol of peace. Some make offerings to Lemanjá, the goddess of the sea, by throwing flowers into the water. Many more come to watch fireworks displays. ✳

The music of Carnaval

LUCCA'S FREE TiME

To: The Reader

Subject: My Free Time

We have a lot of tall buildings where I live. Most of the buildings have soccer fields, some of which are concrete, or swimming pools. Most of the time, I play soccer there with my friends. Most of them live in the building, but others are from school.

In Brazil, most of the people play soccer from the time they are born. We have some organized teams in clubs, but it's really hard to get a place in them. We are supposed to play with our same age group, but some people use fake IDs to play at a younger age, so that means I can't play as much.

Each school has a team, too.

To: The Reader

Subject: My Free Time

We go out at night like kids in the US do, but we don't have lots of outdoor areas like shopping streets. Instead we often go to indoor shopping malls. We can find something to eat and see our friends.

We go to the beach all year, because the water is really warm. I was very surprised when I found how cold the water is on the [North American] West Coast. But I learned to surf there and I was able to surf when I came to Santa Barbara. It was a way to meet new people, too.

My club is called Bahia, the same club that I used to play with. I cheer for the senior team that plays in the national league of Brazil.

Brazil's Economy and Politics

The Brazilian economy is the largest in South America and according to some sources ranks as high as sixth worldwide. Many economists predict it will soon overtake France in the world rankings.

Brazil's economy has gone through several changes. In the colonial era, sugar and cotton were the country's main exports. The establishment of immense coffee plantations in the 19th century soon made coffee the country's primary export. By 1900, half the coffee production in the world came from Brazil.

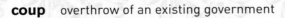

Words to Understand

coup   overthrow of an existing government

impeached   charged a public official with misconduct

inflation   a sudden rise in the general cost of goods or the value of money

infrastructure   physical structures such as buildings and roads essential to the functioning of a nation

plethora   a large amount

Coffee is one of Brazil's most important and famous crops. The fruit of the plant, shown here, was to be opened to reveal the seeds that are made into coffee.

Starting in the late 1960s, the country underwent what was called the "Brazilian Miracle." By then the country had become an urban rather than rural society, with two-thirds of the population living in cities (today that figure is about 85 percent). With so many more potential workers, the government increased its participation in the economy, investing heavily in **infrastructure** and industrial products for export. For several years the economy grew at an annual rate of more than 10 percent. However, the country needed huge amounts of imported oil to fuel its factories. Two oil crises during the 1970s forced the government to borrow large sums of money, leading to years of recession and high rates of **inflation**.

Brazil's Work Force

Today, about 15 percent of Brazil's work force is engaged in agriculture. Brazil is sometimes called "the world's food basket" because it is one of the world's largest exporters of agricultural products. Products such as sugar cane, soybeans, and coffee are distributed worldwide. Beef is also a major source of farm-related income.

Another 15 percent or so work in industry. Mining is an important element of this sector, with the country serving as a source of metals such as iron ore, copper, bauxite, aluminum, and gold. Other major industries include petroleum processing, automobile manufacturing, iron and steel production, and food and beverages. Brazil is also important in the aerospace industry, with Embraer regional jets leading the way. The name stands for Empresa Brasileira de Aeronáutica S.A., and the company is not only the world's largest producer of small planes (37–120 passengers) but also ranks third overall behind industry giants Boeing and Airbus.

The remainder, some 70 percent of all jobs, are in the service sector. This includes everything related to tourism—hotels, guides, travel agents, restaurants, etc.—retail sales, personal services, bureaucrats at every level of government, and hospitality. Financial services are an especially important part of this sector.

Income Inequality

Unfortunately, not everyone shares in such a robust economy. Brazil has one of the greatest differences in income between the wealthy and the poor. According to reliable estimates, the top 10 percent of the population controls about half the country's annual income, while the lowest 10 percent has less than one percent. More than 20 percent of the population lives below the poverty line.

Many impoverished people live in *favelas*, or slums, clustered on the outskirts of many cities. They originated in the late 1800s when soldiers camped on hillsides covered with thorny favela plants. As Brazil's population grew and many people moved to the cities with little money, they had to live in flimsy slapdash dwellings packed tightly together with no sanitation or running water. Rio de Janeiro alone has more than 1,000 favelas. Not surprisingly, they have become hotbeds for drugs and crime.

Dozens of these favelas are located in Rio and other major cities. The tiny houses are packed tightly into hillside areas with little or no water or sanitation.

One unfortunate result is that Brazil has one of the highest murder rates of any country in the world, about 21 per 100,000 people. That's more than three times the worldwide average. Only a handful of cases are ever solved. That rate cuts up to seven years off life expectancy in the favelas.

To help deal with the situation, Brazil launched the Bolsa Familia program in 2003. The country's poorest families receive small cash payments by satisfying certain conditions, such as regular school attendance

Getúlio Vargas ruled as a kind of dictator of Brazil in the 1930s and 1940s. He changed laws so that he was placed in almost total charge.

and preventive health care visits. The program now reaches about one-fourth of the population and has more than halved the number of people in extreme poverty. They also gain self-respect and can offer children a way out of the cycle of poverty. The World Bank, which helped fund the program, plans on using it as a model throughout the world.

Changing Governments

Brazil's government has undergone a number of changes from the down-fall of Pedro II to the present day. The republic established by the military suffered from political instability. While Brazil had regular elections to elect a president and members of congress, the real power lay with people in rural areas, especially the large coffee-growers. That made the country difficult to govern since each region had its own agenda. Brazil had 13 different presidents between 1889 and 1930.

In 1930, the military staged a peaceful **coup** and installed Getúlio Vargas as president. He ruled as a virtual dictator with his primary support coming from the big cities. While he enacted some much-needed reforms, he also rewrote the constitution in his favor and canceled elections. He remained in power until the end of World War II in 1945. Once again the military intervened and Eurico Dutra became president. He later oversaw the writing of a new constitution that called for free elections.

In an odd twist, in 1951 Vargas won the first election under the new constitution. But this time he didn't have his former absolute power. His administration was marked by corruption, scandals, and high levels of inflation. Faced with mounting pressure to resign, he committed suicide.

His successors launched massive building programs, but couldn't stop inflation or political infighting. In 1964, yet again the military staged a coup. Yet again Brazil became a dictatorship, this time led by a series of generals who were initially popular due to the economic boom in the

1970s. But when the boom cooled, public discontent increased. The military allowed free elections in 1985 and returned the country to civilian control. Brazil continued to face enormous economic problems and several presidents struggled to control the situation.

By the early 2000s, the presidency seemed to have finally stabilized. But shortly after Dilma Rousseff was elected in 2010—and thereby became Brazil's first female president—she became involved in a number of controversies. By late 2015, her approval rating dipped to 9 percent. She was **impeached** the following year and removed from office.

To expand the country away from the populated coast, Brazil moved its capital in 1960 to the newly created city of Brasilia in the Amazon highlands.

Government Structure

Today Brazil is divided into 26 states and the Federal District (similar to Washington, D.C.). It has the same type of democratic government as the United States:

- Executive branch headed by an elected president, who can serve two four-year terms and is responsible for appointing cabinet officers.

- National Congress, consisting of the 81-seat Federal Senate with three senators from each state and the Federal District who serve eight-year terms, and 513-seat Chamber of Deputies, with members elected on a proportional basis depending on the size of their respective states and serving for four years.

- Judiciary, with the Brazilian Supreme Federal Tribunal as the country's highest court. It has 11 members and in 2002 became the world's first supreme court to televise its proceedings. Unlike justices in the United States, who are appointed to lifetime terms, Brazilian justices must retire when they reach the age of 75. ✳

Voting in Brazil

The voting age in Brazil is 16. Voting between the ages of 16 to 18, as well as 70 and over, is voluntary. Everyone else, between 18 and 70 is required to vote, or show a good reason if they cannot. Living outside the country is not an acceptable excuse. They must still report to the nearest embassy to cast their ballots. As a result, election turnouts in Brazil routinely are well over 80 percent, compared to the United States where the typical turnout is in the low 50 percent range. Nonvoters may encounter difficulty in seeking a passport or obtaining credit. There are at least 30 political parties from which to choose. That **plethora** means that a single party rarely wins a majority. Instead, a coalition of several parties must form a government.

 BRAZIL

LUCCA'S COUNTRY

To: The Reader

Subject: My country

There is a very big difference between classes of people in Brazil. When I was in the US, I saw that even people who do not have a lot of money can still have a place to live and even have a car. In Brazil, most of the time, there are people with money and very poor people. There is very little middle class in Brazil.

If I walk in my neighborhood, it's pretty safe. But if I go to my school or my friends' house, you have to be very cautious and look around carefully.

The problem in Brazil that I've seen my whole life is that Brazil has a lot of corruption. A lot. So most of the people in government are stealing money and are greedy. We are frustrated that we can't seem to change that. We know there is a lot of it going on. But the government stays in power by telling the poor people that they will help them, so they get the votes. But the [officials] don't do what they say they will do, they don't help them.

"In Brazil, most of the time, there are people with money and very poor people. There is very little middle class in Brazil."

I think something is going to change. When I was young, I never saw people protesting against our government. Now you see that more and more. I remember one time I was playing soccer on a field, but on all the buildings you could see signs of protest and you saw people yelling and cheering protesters and demonstrations. It seems like more people are taking a stand to make things change.

BRAZIL

The Future of Brazil

"**B**razil is the country of the future…and always will be," said French president Charles de Gaulle when Brazil's economy began taking off in the 1960s. But since then, a series of economic and political upheavals has created uncertainty about that future. On one hand, the country has had to deal with abnormally high rates of inflation and stagnation in some of its major trading partners. On the other hand, Brazil remains rich in mineral and agricultural resources as well as an abundant workforce. And the construction of Brasilia from scratch points to the country's ability to create something if it wants to badly enough.

One of the chief challenges facing Brazil as it looks forward is income inequality. There is some evidence that the disparity between rich and poor is being reduced, though the extent of that reduction is not clear.

Words to Understand

coalition   in government, a collection of like-minded groups that govern together

ecotourists   tourists who seek to preserve the environment and the well-being of people who live there

In response to news that their president might be involved in corruption, millions of people took to the streets in Brazil to protest.

One thing does seem clear. The country's education system needs improvement, because ill-performing schools reduce opportunities for economic advancement. There is a wider gap in reading and math scores between children from the uppermost and lowermost families than in most other countries with similar income levels. The continued existence of this gap results in a cycle of poverty, crime, and hopelessness. Many people are especially concerned about a recent constitutional amendment that caps federal spending—meaning less money for education and other pressing issues.

Two other factors must be addressed. One is widespread governmental corruption. This is due in part of the large number of political parties. To form a governing coalition, a series of deals involving bribery and kickbacks is often negotiated among members of the various parties. The other is a network of complex regulations regarding business, especially smaller ones. This can harm individual enterprise.

The country took a step toward fixing some of that when President Dilma Rousseff was impeached (voted out of office before her term was up) in 2016. Millions of people had protested during the debate, showing new signs of becoming engaged in politics. New leadership might help, but Brazil has serious economic problems to deal with including high unemployment and low growth.

The Future of the Rainforest

Economics and politics aside, nothing is more important for Brazil's future—and the future of the world— than the Amazon rainforest. Its sheer size exerts a major influence in stabilizing the climate, both in Brazil and around the world. Unfortunately, the worldwide increase in demand for beef and agricultural products has resulted in massive land clearing because much of the best land for growing crops and raising meat animals lies in the Amazon Basin. According to estimates, nearly three million acres of rain forest (4,500 square miles, an area the size of Delaware and Rhode Island combined) are chopped down every year. Some estimates are that the rainforest could completely disappear in less than 50 years at the current rate of destruction.

Some people benefit financially. Logging and ranching provide livelihoods for many Brazilians and their families. But the new roads that make it easier to access the interior and thereby facilitate getting agricultural products to market make it easier for illegal loggers to operate. Large-scale farming also displaces smaller farmers, who in turn clear additional land as they seek new places to settle.

How Brazil protects its massive rainforest while also trying to take advantage of its resources will play a big role in the country's economic future.

Environmental Dangers

The rainforest contains vast amounts of carbon. Cutting down forests may release this carbon into the atmosphere. In addition, 30 million people live there and rely on the continued health of the rainforest for their livelihood, food, and housing. Many rare plants found only in the rainforest are used to make beneficial drugs and for medical treatments. When the rainforest is gone, so are they. In addition, excessive exploitation of natural resources—often with little regard for the environment—leads to soil erosion and contamination of the water.

Brazil is fighting against the massive clear-cutting of irreplaceable rainforest. Scenes like this one are rallying an international force to save the land.

Massive dams such as this one on the Tocantins River in north-central Brazil provide much-needed power, but can have effects on the rainforest.

In addition, the Brazilian constitution recognizes the right of indigenous people to live on their traditional lands and pursue their long-established way of life. But the exploitation of the rainforest ignores this right. The government must somehow retain their culture while introducing them into the modern era.

Dams

The Amazon River itself and its tributaries are subject to another danger. As Brazil continues to modernize and provide more amenities for its people, there is an increasing demand for power. As a result, a number of dams are either under construction or in the planning stages. While these dams provide much-needed power, they disturb the flow of the river. This

Lucca on Faith in Brazil

In Brazil, most of the people believe in God and most of the people are Catholic. We are Catholics, but we don't go to the churches—actually, my grand-mother goes every Sunday!

disturbance can harm many aquatic species as well as interfere with fishing.

One response to rainforest loss is governmental emphasis on increasing the numbers of **ecotourists** who visit the country. According to a recent report, one-fifth of foreigners travel to Brazil because of the opportunities in ecotourism (though not surprisingly, the majority—more than 60 percent—are attracted primarily by the country's beach culture and the chance to kick back and relax in the sun).

Studies indicate that ecotourists spend as much as four times more than conventional tourists. One goal is to use revenue generated by ecotourism

In terms of population, Brazil is the largest Catholic country in the world. Its faithful were thrilled by the visit of Pope Francis I, who is from nearby Argentina.

to ease the economic impact on those displaced by deforestation and perhaps slow it down.

Will Brazil Remain Roman Catholic?

Another development is that while Brazil is still the home to the largest number of Roman Catholics in the world, the actual percentage has decreased sharply in recent years. The 2010 census indicates that fewer than 65 percent of Brazilians consider themselves Catholic, down from more than 90 percent in 1970.

This trend is especially evident among young people. Many of those leaving the Catholic faith embrace Protestantism, while others have no religious affiliation. Brazilian Cardinal Cláudio Hummes said, "We wonder with anxiety: how long will Brazil remain a Catholic country?" *

Catholics in Brazil

The Future of Soccer

Because of the supreme value that Brazilians place on soccer, how well their national team plays is vitally important. The 7-1 loss to Germany in the 2014 World Cup was especially disheartening. It didn't help that Brazil was eliminated in the group stage of the 2016 Copa América—which matches teams from North, Central, and South America—shortly before the Olympics. Many people—inside the country and outside observers—said that the team had abandoned the fluid style of play that was so characteristic of Brazilian soccer. Making things even worse, several top Brazilian soccer officials were convicted of corruption charges. But the Olympic gold medal showcased a number of young stars and helped make up for the previous defeats. Brazilians look forward to the 2018 World Cup in Russia and hope that the team will notch its sixth title.

 BRAZIL

 # TEXT-DEPENDENT QUESTIONS

1. What language do Brazilians speak?

2. What is Brazil's soccer-related nickname?

3. What are some of Brazil's most important industries?

4. What is Carnaval?

5. Why is there some concern for the future of Catholicism in Brazil?

6. What president was impeached in 2016?

7. What does Lucca say is one of the biggest problems in Brazil?

8. What are some of the consequences of rainforest destruction?

RESEARCH PROJECTS

1. Read more about the life and accomplishments of Pelé and the effect he had on soccer in the United States.

2. See how the Gracie family helped introduce MMA to a much wider audience.

3. Choose an animal living in the Amazon Basin and find out more about it. Another idea is to look into how a rainforest is organized. Read about the different levels and then design a poster to show how those levels are arranged.

4. Discover the history and construction of the Christ the Redeemer statue that towers above Rio de Janeiro.

5. Read more about the 2016 presidential crisis in Brazil. What are people saying will happen to the country in the future?

FIND OUT MORE

Books

Branco, Sandra. *Brazil: The Essential Guide to Customs and Culture.* London: Kuperard, 2014.

Goldblatt, David. *Futebol Nation: The Story of Brazil Through Soccer.* New York: Nation Books, 2014.

Hinchberger, Bill. *National Geographic Traveler: Brazil.* Washington, DC: National Geographic, 2014.

Richard, Christopher and Leslie Jermyn. *Cultures of the World: Brazil.* Tarrytown, NY: Benchmark Books, 2002.

Websites

https://www.cia.gov/library/publications/resources/the-world-factbook/geos/br.html
Overview of Brazil with brief descriptions of its government, economy, people, geography, and more.

www.worldbank.org/en/country/brazil/overview
The economy of Brazil will be a major story for years to come. This site from the World Bank gives a wide overview of the numbers.

bleacherreport.com/brazilian-football
Follow the action and the stars of Brazil's national team, as well as updates on the senior pro league there, on this sports site.

SERIES GLOSSARY OF KEY TERMS

arable land   land suitable for cultivation and the growing of crops

commodity   a raw material that has value and is regularly bought and sold

cuisine   cooking that is characteristic of a particular country, region, or restaurant

destabilize   damage, disrupt, undermine

dynasties   long periods of time during which one extended family rules a place

industrialization   the process in which an economy is transformed from mainly agricultural to one based on manufacturing goods

infrastructure   buildings, roads, services, and other things that are necessary for a society to function

lunar calendar   a calendar based on the period from one moon to the next. Each cycle is 28 1/2 to 29 days, so the lunar year is about 354 days

parliamentary   describes a government in which a body of cabinet ministers is chosen from the legislature and act as advisers to the chief of state (or prime minister)

resonate   echo and reverberate; stay current through time

sovereignty   having supreme power and authority

venerate   treat with great respect

INDEX

Photo Credits

Adobe Images: sfmthd 15, picsfive 19b, markos86 25. Alamy Stock: Lanmas 13, Edward Parker 57. AP Images: Roy K. Miller/Icon Sportswire 41b. Dreamstime.com: Celso Diniz 9, Pixattitude 9, 23, 30t, Tony Bosse 11, William87 18, Antonio Diaz 19t, Paul Brighton 20, Luiz Ribeiro 21, Marchello74 26, Dndavis 27, Leon Viti 30t, Anky10 30b, Edward Marques-Mortimer 33, Luizsouzari 36, Aguina 37, 38, Alfoto 43, Dabldy 45, 53, Filipe Frazao 48, 55, Tupungato 50l, sjors737 50r, Henrique Araujo 51b, TravelStrategy 56, Marilia Kimie Shimabukuro 58. Ensinar Historia: 35. Eric Isaacs: 8. Newscom: Brian Kersey/UPI 16; Shutterstock: Brazilphoto 40. Wikiwand: 14, 46.

Author

Jim Whiting has published more than 180 nonfiction books for young readers. He is the most prolific author in his home state of Washington. His subjects literally run the gamut from A(ntarctica) to Z(ionism). His goal is to write a stack of books taller than he is. Right now the level is at his collarbone.